Maximizing KDP Sales with ChatGPT

A Side Hustle Guide

Strellus

1. Introduction to ChatGPT and its capabilities for KDP authors
2. Idea Generation: Using ChatGPT to spark creative ideas for your book
3. Research: Using ChatGPT for market and audience research
4. Keyword Optimization: Using ChatGPT to identify and target the right keywords for your book
5. Writing the Book Description: Using ChatGPT to write compelling and effective book descriptions
6. Crafting the Title: Using ChatGPT to come up with catchy and attention-grabbing titles
7. Writing the Book: Using ChatGPT to generate outlines, write content and even entire books
8. Optimizing for SEO: Using ChatGPT to include keywords and improve search visibility
9. Promotions and Marketing: Using ChatGPT to write ads, social media posts and other promotions
10. Conclusion: Putting it all together - using ChatGPT to take your KDP side hustle to the next level
11. How to Guide: Use ChatGPT to create KDP book listings

Introduction to ChatGPT and its capabilities for KDP authors

ChatGPT, or Generative Pre-training Transformer, is a state-of-the-art language model developed by OpenAI. It is capable of understanding and generating natural language text with an unprecedented level of accuracy and fluency. The model is trained on a massive dataset of text from the internet, giving it a deep understanding of the nuances and complexities of human language.

At its core, ChatGPT is a machine learning algorithm that uses deep neural networks to generate text. It uses a technique called unsupervised learning, which means that it learns from the data it is given without any explicit guidance or labels. This allows it to generate text that is similar in style and content to the text it has seen during its training phase.

One of the most striking features of ChatGPT is its ability to understand and respond to context. This means that it can generate text that is not only grammatically correct but also semantically coherent. For example, if you prompt ChatGPT with the sentence "The cat sat on the mat," it can generate a follow-up sentence that is coherent and relevant, such as "The mat was soft and fluffy."

ChatGPT's capabilities are not limited to understanding and generating text, it can also be used to perform other natural language processing tasks such as language translation, text summarization, and sentiment analysis.

The capabilities of ChatGPT make it an extremely powerful tool for KDP authors. With its ability to generate high-quality text, it can help authors write better book descriptions, captivating titles and even entire books. For example, it can be used to generate ideas for books, create outlines, and write content that will sell your books.

In summary, ChatGPT is a state-of-the-art language model that can understand and generate natural language text with an unprecedented level of accuracy and fluency. It is trained on a massive dataset of text from the internet, giving it a deep understanding of the nuances and complexities of human language. It can be used to perform a variety of natural language processing tasks, making it an extremely powerful tool for KDP authors.

How ChatGPT can benefit KDP authors

ChatGPT can benefit KDP authors in a number of ways, making it an essential tool for anyone looking to boost their self-publishing success. Some of the key ways that ChatGPT can help authors include:

1. Writing Better Book Descriptions: One of the most important elements of selling a book is the book description. It's the first thing that potential buyers will read, and it needs to be compelling, accurate and informative. ChatGPT can help authors write book descriptions that are engaging and accurate, by analyzing the book content and generate a summary of it.

2. Generating Captivating Book Titles: A catchy and memorable title can be the difference between a book that sells and one that doesn't. ChatGPT can help authors come up with titles that are both memorable and relevant to the book's content.

3. Writing Entire Books: ChatGPT can also help authors write entire books, by suggesting ideas, creating outlines, and even writing content. This can save authors a lot of time and effort, and help them produce higher-quality work.

4. Language Translation: ChatGPT can also be used to translate books into other languages, making them more accessible to readers around the world. This can help authors reach a wider audience and increase sales.

5. Text Summarization: ChatGPT can help authors to summarize long texts into shorter and more concise versions, making them more accessible to readers with limited time and attention span.

6. Sentiment Analysis: ChatGPT can help authors to understand the sentiment or tone of their text, whether it's positive, negative or neutral, this can help authors to adjust their writing style and messages to better connect with their audience.

In summary, ChatGPT is a powerful tool that can help KDP authors in a number of ways. From writing better book descriptions, to generating captivating book titles, and even writing entire books, ChatGPT can help authors produce higher-quality work and reach a wider audience. Additionally, it can be used for language translation, text summarization and sentiment analysis which makes the text more accessible and better tailored to the audience.

Creating compelling book descriptions with ChatGPT

A book's description is a crucial part of the self-publishing process, as it's the first thing that potential buyers will read. A well-written and engaging book description can entice readers to purchase a book, while a poorly written one can deter them. ChatGPT can help authors write compelling book descriptions by analyzing the book content and generating a summary of it.

To use ChatGPT to write a book description, authors can start by providing the model with a summary of the book's plot and main characters. ChatGPT will then analyze the text and generate a summary of it that is both accurate and engaging. The generated text can be used as a starting point for the book description, which the author can then edit and refine as needed.

One of the key benefits of using ChatGPT for book descriptions is that it can save authors a lot of time and effort. Instead of spending hours trying to come up with the perfect words to describe their book, authors can let ChatGPT do the heavy lifting and then simply edit the generated text as needed.

Another benefit is that ChatGPT can help authors write book descriptions that are both accurate and engaging. The model has been trained on a massive dataset of text from the internet, giving it a deep understanding of the nuances and complexities of human language. This means that it can generate text that is not only grammatically correct but also semantically coherent. The generated text also can be tailored to the author's target audience, which can increase the chances of making a sale.

In addition to generating a summary of the book's plot and main characters, ChatGPT can also be used to write other elements of a book description, such as the book's genre, themes, and tone. This can help authors create a well-rounded and engaging book description that will entice readers to purchase their book.

In summary, ChatGPT can help authors write compelling book descriptions by analyzing the book content and generating a summary of it. This can save authors a lot of time and effort, and help them produce a high-quality book description that is both accurate and engaging. The generated text also can be tailored to the author's target audience, which can increase the chances of making a sale. Additionally, ChatGPT can be used to write other elements of a book description, such as the book's genre, themes, and tone. This can help authors create a well-rounded and engaging book description that will entice readers to purchase their book.

Generating captivating book titles using ChatGPT

A catchy and memorable book title can be the difference between a book that sells and one that doesn't. ChatGPT can help authors come up with titles that are both memorable and relevant to the book's content.

To use ChatGPT to generate book titles, authors can start by providing the model with a summary of the book's plot and main characters. ChatGPT will then analyze the text and generate a list of potential titles that are relevant to the book's content. The generated titles can be used as a starting point for the author to choose from and refine as needed.

One of the key benefits of using ChatGPT for book titles is that it can save authors a lot of time and effort. Instead of spending hours trying to come up with the perfect title, authors can let ChatGPT do the heavy lifting and then simply choose from the generated options.

Another benefit is that ChatGPT can help authors come up with titles that are both memorable and relevant to the book's content. The model has been trained on a massive dataset of text from the internet, giving it a deep understanding of the nuances and complexities of human language. This means that it can generate titles that are not only catchy but also semantically coherent with the book's content.

Additionally, ChatGPT can generate titles that are tailored to the author's target audience, which can increase the chances of making a sale. For example, if the author's target audience is young adults, ChatGPT can generate titles that are relatable and appealing to that age group.

Authors can also use ChatGPT to generate a list of alternative titles for their book. This can be useful when authors want to test different titles to see which one resonates best with readers. Having a list of alternative titles also can be useful when the author's first choice is not available for use.

In summary, ChatGPT can help authors generate captivating book titles by analyzing the book's content and generating a list of potential titles that are both memorable and relevant to the book's content. This can save authors a lot of time and effort and help them come up with titles that are tailored to the author's target audience, which can increase the chances of making a sale. Additionally, ChatGPT can generate a list of alternative titles for the author to choose from, this can be useful when authors want to test different titles or when the first choice is not available for use.

Writing entire books with the help of ChatGPT

ChatGPT can also help authors write entire books, by suggesting ideas, creating outlines, and even writing content. This can save authors a lot of time and effort and help them produce higher-quality work.

To use ChatGPT to write an entire book, authors can start by providing the model with a summary of the book's plot and main characters. ChatGPT will then analyze the text and generate a list of potential ideas for the book, based on the provided information. The generated ideas can be used as a starting point for the author to choose from and develop further.

One of the key benefits of using ChatGPT for book writing is that it can save authors a lot of time and effort. Instead of spending hours trying to come up with ideas and writing content, authors can let ChatGPT do the heavy lifting and then simply edit the generated text as needed.

Another benefit is that ChatGPT can help authors write content that is both accurate and engaging. The model has been trained on a massive dataset of text from the internet, giving it a deep understanding of the nuances and complexities of human language. This means that it can generate text that is not only grammatically correct but also semantically coherent and tailored to the author's target audience.

Additionally, ChatGPT can help authors create an outline for their book. By providing the model with a summary of the book's plot and main characters,

ChatGPT can generate a list of potential chapter titles and summaries. This can help authors to organize their thoughts and structure their book in a logical way.

Authors can also use ChatGPT to write specific scenes or chapters of their book. For example, if an author is struggling to write a particular scene, they can provide ChatGPT with the context and characters involved in that scene and the model will generate text for the scene.

In summary, ChatGPT can help authors write entire books by suggesting ideas, creating outlines, and even writing content. This can save authors a lot of time and effort and help them produce higher-quality work. Additionally, ChatGPT can help authors write content that is both accurate and engaging and tailored to the author's target audience. It can also help authors create an outline for their book and write specific scenes or chapters of their book. This feature of ChatGPT can be extremely helpful for authors who are struggling with writer's block or want to improve the quality of their work.

Idea Generation: Using ChatGPT to spark creative ideas for your book

Understanding the power of ChatGPT for idea generation and how it can help authors overcome writer's block

One of the most powerful features of ChatGPT is its ability to generate ideas. As a language model, it has been trained on a vast amount of text data, which allows it to understand and generate a wide range of concepts and ideas. This makes it an invaluable tool for authors looking to overcome writer's block and generate new and exciting story concepts.

One of the key advantages of using ChatGPT for idea generation is that it can help you think outside the box. By providing you with a wide range of potential ideas, it can help you break out of familiar patterns and come up with new and unique concepts. Additionally, because it can generate a wide range of different types of ideas, it can be used in all stages of the writing process, from brainstorming to outlining and even writing entire passages of text.

Another great benefit of using ChatGPT for idea generation is that it can help you conduct research and gather inspiration for your book. By providing you with a wide range of potential ideas, it can help you understand the market and what kind of concepts are currently popular. Additionally, you can use it to gather inspiration from other books, movies, or other media to help you come up with new and unique ideas.

To get the most out of ChatGPT for idea generation, it's important to understand how it works. The model uses a process called "completion" to generate text, based on the input provided. To generate ideas, you can provide it with a prompt or a seed text, and then ask it to complete it. The generated text will be based on the input, but it will also include new and original ideas that you can use in your book.

In conclusion, using ChatGPT for idea generation is a powerful tool that can help authors overcome writer's block and generate new and exciting story concepts. Its ability to generate a wide range of ideas, and to conduct research and gather inspiration makes it an invaluable tool for the writing process. Understanding how to use it effectively and providing it with good prompts will help you get the most out of it.

Tips for using ChatGPT to generate a wide range of ideas, from plotlines to character names and more

Using ChatGPT for idea generation is a powerful tool that can help authors generate a wide range of ideas. From plotlines and character names to settings and themes, ChatGPT can help you come up with new and exciting concepts for your book.

One way to use ChatGPT for idea generation is by providing it with a specific prompt or seed text that relates to the type of idea you're looking for. For example, if you're looking to generate ideas for a new plotline, you can provide ChatGPT with a prompt like "What if a detective solves a crime and finds out the criminal is his long-lost twin brother?" and ask it to complete it. This will provide you with a wide range of potential plot ideas that you can use as the basis for your story. Similarly, you can provide it with a prompt like "What if a person wakes up one day with the ability to time travel?" and ask it to complete it to get ideas for science fiction story.

Another way to use ChatGPT for idea generation is by using it to generate a list of character names, settings, or themes. For example, you can provide it with a prompt like "Generate a list of names for characters in a fantasy story" and ask it to complete it. This will provide you with a list of potential character names that you can use in your story. Similarly, you can provide it with a prompt like "Generate a list of settings for a horror story" and ask it to complete it, to get ideas for potential settings for your story.

Another technique is to use ChatGPT to generate random and creative ideas. You can provide it with a prompt like "Generate an idea for a story" and ask it to complete it. This can provide you with a wide range of unexpected and unique ideas that can be used as the basis for your story.

In addition to providing you with a wide range of ideas, using ChatGPT for idea generation can also help you overcome writer's block. By providing you with a wide range of potential ideas, it can help you break out of familiar patterns and come up with new and unique concepts. Additionally, because it can generate a wide range of different types of ideas, it can be used in all stages of the writing process, from brainstorming to outlining and even writing entire passages of text.

In conclusion, using ChatGPT for idea generation is a powerful tool that can help authors generate a wide range of ideas from plotlines and character names to settings and themes. It's a great way to overcome writer's block, and to come up with new and exciting concepts for your story. By providing it with good prompts, you can get a wide range of ideas that can be used as the basis for your book.

Techniques for using ChatGPT to brainstorm and develop unique and compelling story concepts

Using ChatGPT to brainstorm and develop unique and compelling story concepts is one of the most powerful ways to take advantage of its capabilities. The model's ability to understand and generate a wide range of concepts allows it to provide a wealth of ideas and inspiration to help authors take their story concepts to the next level.

One of the key techniques for using ChatGPT to brainstorm and develop unique and compelling story concepts is to provide it with a general prompt or seed text that describes the basic idea of the story you want to write. For example, you might provide a prompt like "A group of friends go on a camping trip and stumble upon a mysterious and dangerous creature." ChatGPT will then generate a list of potential plotlines, character names, and other story elements that you can use as inspiration for your story.

Another technique for using ChatGPT to develop unique and compelling story concepts is to provide it with a list of specific story elements that you want to include in your story. For example, you might provide a list of character names and ask ChatGPT to generate a plotline that includes all of them. This can be a great way to come up with new and original ideas for your story.

It's also important to experiment with different types of prompts and seed texts to see what kind of ideas ChatGPT generates. For example, you might try providing a list of keywords and asking ChatGPT to generate a story that includes all of them, or you might try providing a short passage of text and asking ChatGPT to generate a story that continues it. Experimentation is key to finding the right prompts that work best for you and your story.

Another technique to consider is to use ChatGPT to generate character and setting descriptions. Characters are the heart of any story, and ChatGPT can help you create characters that are unique, relatable and believable. With its ability to understand and generate human-like text, ChatGPT can help you create complex, multi-dimensional characters that will make your story stand out.

In conclusion, using ChatGPT to brainstorm and develop unique and compelling story concepts is a powerful way to take advantage of its capabilities. By providing it with prompts and seed texts, you can generate a wide range of ideas and inspiration that can help you take your story concepts to the next level. Experimentation and providing different types of prompts can help you find the right approach that works best for you and your story.

Best practices for using ChatGPT to conduct research and gather inspiration for your book ideas

One of the best practices when using ChatGPT for idea generation is to conduct research and gather inspiration for your book. This is important to help you understand the market, what kind of concepts are currently popular and how to create a story that will stand out. By providing ChatGPT with a wide range of information about your book's topic, you can help it generate ideas that are relevant, engaging and marketable.

There are several ways to gather information and inspiration for your book when using ChatGPT. One of the most effective is to read other books in your genre. By understanding the themes, characters, and plotlines of other successful books, you can get a sense of what is working in the market and use that information to inform your own story. Additionally, you can use ChatGPT to analyze these books and extract key information, such as common themes, character traits, and plot structures.

Another great way to gather inspiration for your book is to use ChatGPT to analyze movies, TV shows, and other media in your genre. By understanding the themes, characters, and plotlines of these popular stories, you can get a sense of what is working in the market and use that information to inform your own story. Additionally, you can use ChatGPT to extract key information, such as common themes, character traits, and plot structures.

You can also use ChatGPT to gather information and inspiration from real-world events, such as news articles and historical events. By understanding the themes, characters, and plotlines of these real-world stories, you can get a sense of what is working in the market and use that information to inform your own story. Additionally, you can use ChatGPT to extract key information, such as common themes, character traits, and plot structures.

Another great way to gather inspiration for your book is to use ChatGPT to conduct research on the target audience of your book. By understanding their interests, demographics, and reading habits, you can create a story that will be highly engaging for them. Additionally, you can use ChatGPT to analyze feedback from readers and use that information to improve your book.

In conclusion, gathering information and inspiration for your book is an important step when using ChatGPT for idea generation. By providing ChatGPT with a wide range of information about your book's topic, you can help it generate ideas that are relevant, engaging and marketable. Reading other books in your genre, analyzing movies, TV shows, and other media, gathering information and inspiration from real-world events, and conducting research on the target audience are some of the ways to gather information and inspiration. This will help you create a story that will stand out in the market and connect with readers.

How to use ChatGPT to evaluate and refine your ideas, to ensure they are marketable and engaging for your target audience

Once you've generated a list of ideas using ChatGPT, it's important to evaluate and refine them to ensure they are marketable and engaging for your target audience. One of the key benefits of using ChatGPT for this process is that it can help you understand the potential of each idea and how it might be received by readers.

One way to evaluate and refine your ideas is by using ChatGPT to conduct market research. By providing it with your ideas and asking it to generate text based on them, you can get a sense of how similar concepts have been received in the past. Additionally, you can use ChatGPT to understand the current trends in your genre or niche, which can help you identify which ideas are more likely to be successful.

Another way to refine your ideas is by using ChatGPT to conduct audience research. By providing it with your ideas and asking it to generate text from the perspective of your target audience, you can get a sense of how they might respond to your concepts. This can help you identify which ideas are more likely to resonate with your audience and which ones might need more work.

Once you've evaluated and refined your ideas, you can use ChatGPT to help you develop a more detailed outline for your book. By providing it with your ideas and asking it to generate a plot outline or character arcs, you can get a sense of how your story might unfold. Additionally, you can use ChatGPT to generate a list of potential themes, symbols or motifs that you can use to make your story more rich and engaging.

Another way to use ChatGPT in this stage is by providing it with your refined ideas and asking it to generate a summary or pitch for the book. This can help you understand how to market and promote your book effectively. Additionally, you can use ChatGPT to generate sample chapters or book reviews to get a sense of how your book will be perceived by readers.

In conclusion, evaluating and refining your ideas using ChatGPT is a powerful way to ensure that your book will be marketable and engaging for your target audience. The ability to conduct market and audience research, develop detailed outlines, generate summaries and pitches, and even sample chapters and reviews make ChatGPT a valuable tool to help you take your ideas to the next level and make them more polished and ready to be sold.

Research: Using ChatGPT for market and audience research

The importance of market and audience research in the book writing process and how ChatGPT can assist with it

Market and audience research are crucial steps in the book writing process, as they can help authors understand what readers want and what the competition is like in their genre or niche. Without this knowledge, it can be difficult to write a book that will be well-received by readers and stand out in a crowded market. ChatGPT can assist with this process by providing authors with a wide range of data and insights that can help them make informed decisions about their book.

One of the key benefits of using ChatGPT for market research is its ability to analyze large amounts of data quickly. By providing it with a list of books or keywords related to your genre or niche, you can ask it to generate a summary of the market and understand the current trends and popular themes. Additionally, you can use ChatGPT to conduct competitor analysis by providing it with the titles of similar books and asking it to generate summaries of their content, themes and target audiences. This can help you identify what sets your book apart and how to position it in the market.

Another great benefit of using ChatGPT for audience research is its ability to analyze customer reviews. By providing it with a list of reviews, it can generate summaries that highlight the most common feedback, whether positive or negative. This can help you understand what readers like and dislike about similar books, and what they are looking for in a book like yours. Additionally, you can use ChatGPT to generate a list of keywords and phrases that are commonly used in the reviews, which can help you identify what readers are looking for in your book.

Moreover, ChatGPT can assist with understanding your target audience by conducting research on demographics and behaviours. By providing it with data on your target audience, you can ask it to generate a summary of the audience's preferences and behaviours, which can help you understand what kind of book they are likely to be interested in. This can help you make informed decisions about your book's themes, characters, and style.

Lastly, using ChatGPT to stay up-to-date with current trends and changes in the publishing industry is another great way to use it. By providing it with keywords related to the industry, you can ask it to generate summaries of the latest news, trends, and changes. This can help you understand what's happening in the industry and how it might affect your book.

In conclusion, using ChatGPT for market and audience research is a powerful way to gain insights and make informed decisions about your book. By providing it with a wide range of data and keywords, you can conduct competitor analysis, understand reader's preferences, understand your target audience and stay up-to-date with current trends and changes in the industry. This will help you create a book that will stand out in the market and be well-received by readers.

Using ChatGPT to conduct research on competitors and similar books in your genre or niche.

Using ChatGPT to conduct research on competitors and similar books in your genre or niche is a powerful way to gain insights and identify opportunities for your own book. By providing it with the titles of similar books and asking it to generate summaries of their content, themes, and target audiences, you can get a sense of what sets your book apart and how to position it in the market.

One of the key benefits of using ChatGPT for competitor research is its ability to analyze large amounts of data quickly. By providing it with the titles of similar books, you can ask it to generate a summary of their themes, plotlines, characters, and target audiences. This can help you understand what readers are looking for in books like yours and how you can differentiate your book from the competition. Additionally, you can use ChatGPT to conduct a SWOT analysis (Strengths, Weaknesses, opportunities, and threats) of your competitors by providing it with the titles of similar books and asking it to generate summaries that include the strengths, weaknesses, opportunities, and threats for each book.

Another way to use ChatGPT for competitor research is by providing it with the titles of similar books and asking it to generate summaries of their reviews. This can help you understand what readers like and dislike about similar books, which can help you identify opportunities to improve your own book. Additionally, you can use ChatGPT to generate a list of keywords and phrases that are commonly used in the reviews, which can help you identify what readers are looking for in your book.

Additionally, you can use ChatGPT to conduct market research by providing it with the titles of similar books and asking it to generate a summary of their sales and revenue. This can help you understand the market potential and competition of your genre or niche.

Moreover, you can use ChatGPT to conduct a research on the authors of similar books. By providing it with the names of the authors, you can ask it to generate a summary of their background, writing style and their previous works. This can help you understand the author's writing style, which can help you position your book accordingly.

In conclusion, using ChatGPT to conduct research on competitors and similar books in your genre or niche is a powerful way to gain insights and identify opportunities for your own book. By providing it with the titles of similar books and asking it to generate summaries of their content, themes, target audiences, reviews, sales, revenue and authors, you can understand the market, the competition, and the readers preferences. This will help you create a book that will stand out in the market and be well-received by readers.

Techniques for using ChatGPT to analyze customer reviews and gather insights on what readers are looking for in a book.

Using ChatGPT to analyze customer reviews is a great way to gather insights on what readers are looking for in a book. Customer reviews can provide valuable feedback on a book's strengths and weaknesses, as well as what readers liked and didn't like about it. By analyzing customer reviews, you can gain a better understanding of what readers are looking for in a book and what they are willing to pay for.

One way to use ChatGPT to analyze customer reviews is by providing it with a list of reviews and asking it to generate a summary of the most common feedback. This can help you understand what readers liked and didn't like about similar books, and what they are looking for in a book like yours. Additionally, you can use ChatGPT to generate a list of keywords and phrases that are commonly used in the reviews, which can help you identify what readers are looking for in your book.

Another way to use ChatGPT for customer review analysis is by providing it with a list of reviews and asking it to generate a sentiment analysis. This can help you understand the overall sentiment of the reviews, whether they are mostly positive or negative. Additionally, you can use ChatGPT to generate a list of keywords and phrases that are associated with positive or negative sentiment, which can help you understand what readers liked and didn't like about similar books.

You can also use ChatGPT to generate a list of common complaints or issues that are mentioned in the reviews. This can help you identify potential weaknesses in your book or areas that you need to work on. Additionally, you can use ChatGPT to generate a list of common praises or positive feedback that are mentioned in the reviews, which can help you identify potential strengths in your book or areas that you should focus on.

Furthermore, ChatGPT can help you understand the demographics of the reviewers by providing it with the reviews and asking it to generate a summary of the reviewers' demographics. This can help you understand the age, gender, location, and other characteristics of the reviewers, which can help you understand your target audience.

In conclusion, using ChatGPT to analyze customer reviews is a powerful way to gather insights on what readers are looking for in a book. By providing it with a list of reviews and asking it to generate summaries, sentiment analysis, common complaints and praises, and demographic analysis, you can gain a better understanding of what readers liked and didn't like about similar books, what they are looking for in a book like yours, and who your target audience is. This information can help you make informed decisions about your book and increase its chances of success.

Using ChatGPT to conduct audience research and understand your target reader's preferences and behaviours.

Using ChatGPT to conduct audience research is an effective way to understand your target readers' preferences and behaviours. By providing it with data on your target audience, you can ask it to generate a summary of their demographics, interests, and habits. This can help you understand what kind of book they are likely to be interested in and how to reach them effectively.

One of the ways to conduct audience research using ChatGPT is by providing it with data about your target audience's demographics, such as age, gender, location, and education level. You can ask it to generate a summary of how these factors might influence their reading habits and preferences. Additionally, you can use ChatGPT to understand your target audience's interests by providing it with keywords related to their hobbies, interests and occupation. It can generate a summary of how these interests might influence their reading preferences and what kind of book they might be interested in.

Another way to conduct audience research using ChatGPT is by providing it with data about your target audience's behaviours, such as reading habits, how they discover new books, and what platforms they use to read. You can ask it to generate a summary of how these behaviours might influence their reading preferences and what kind of book they might be interested in. Additionally, you can use ChatGPT to understand your target audience's preferences by providing it with keywords related to books they have read and liked. It can generate a summary of what kind of books they might be interested in and what themes, characters, and styles they prefer.

You can also use ChatGPT to conduct research on the target audience's pain points, frustrations and problems. By providing it with data about your target audience's pain points and frustrations, you can ask it to generate a summary of how these factors might influence their reading habits and preferences. Additionally, you can use ChatGPT to understand the problems they are facing and what solutions they are looking for by providing it with keywords related to their problems. It can generate a summary of how these problems might influence their reading preferences and what kind of book they might be interested in.

Moreover, you can use ChatGPT to conduct research on how to effectively reach your target audience. By providing it with data on your target audience's behaviours and preferences, you can ask it to generate a summary of the most effective ways to reach them. This can help you understand what kind of marketing and promotion strategies will be most effective for your book.

In conclusion, using ChatGPT to conduct audience research is an effective way to understand your target readers' preferences and behaviours. By providing it with data on your target audience's demographics, interests, behaviours, pain points, and preferences, you can gain insights on what kind of book they are likely to be interested in and how to reach them effectively. Additionally, you can use ChatGPT to understand the problems they are facing and what solutions they are looking for, which can help you to create a book that addresses those issues.

Best practices for using ChatGPT to stay up-to-date with current trends and changes in the publishing industry.

Staying up-to-date with current trends and changes in the publishing industry is essential for any author looking to succeed in the market. The industry is constantly evolving, and it's important to understand how these changes might affect your book. ChatGPT can assist with this process by providing authors with a wide range of data and insights that can help them stay informed and make strategic decisions about their book.

One way to use ChatGPT to stay up-to-date with the industry is by providing it with keywords related to the publishing industry and asking it to generate summaries of the latest news, trends, and changes. This can help you understand what's happening in the industry and how it might affect your book. For example, if you're writing a book in the self-help genre, you can ask ChatGPT to generate summaries about the latest trends in self-help and personal development, which can help you understand what's popular and what readers are looking for in this genre.

Another way to use ChatGPT to stay informed about the industry is by providing it with the names of influential people or organizations in the publishing industry and asking it to generate summaries of their latest statements or publications. This can help you understand the industry's leaders' perspectives and the direction they see the industry going in the future.

Additionally, you can use ChatGPT to generate summaries of recent market reports or studies, which can help you understand the current state of the market and identify new opportunities. For instance, if you're writing a book on a specific sub-genre of fiction, you can ask ChatGPT to generate summaries of recent market reports on that genre, which can help you understand the current state of the market and identify new opportunities within it.

Furthermore, you can use ChatGPT to conduct research on new technologies and platforms that are being used in the publishing industry. For example, you can ask it to generate summaries of the latest developments in e-book formats or audiobook production, which can help you understand how to make your book available in the most current and popular formats.

Lastly, you can use ChatGPT to generate summaries of recent book sales data, which can help you understand what kind of books are selling well in the market and what readers are interested in buying. This can help you identify new opportunities and make strategic decisions about your book.

In conclusion, using ChatGPT to stay up-to-date with current trends and changes in the publishing industry is a powerful way to gain insights and make strategic decisions about your book. By providing it with a wide range of data and keywords, you can understand the latest news, trends, perspectives of industry leaders and recent market reports. This can help you create a book that will be well-received by readers and stand out in the market.

Keyword Optimization: Using ChatGPT to identify and target the right keywords for your book

The importance of keyword optimization in the book marketing process and how ChatGPT can assist with it

Keyword optimization is an essential part of the book marketing process, as it can help increase visibility and drive sales. By identifying and targeting the right keywords for your book, you can improve search engine rankings and make it more likely for readers to find your book. ChatGPT can assist with this process by providing authors with a wide range of data and insights that can help them identify and target the most relevant keywords for their book.

One of the key benefits of using ChatGPT for keyword optimization is its ability to conduct research on the most relevant and high-performing keywords for your book and genre. By providing it with your book's title and description, as well as keywords related to your genre or niche, you can ask it to generate a list of the most relevant keywords and phrases that you should target. Additionally, you can use ChatGPT to conduct competitor analysis by providing it with the titles of similar books and asking it to generate a list of the keywords and phrases that they are targeting. This can help you identify which keywords are most likely to drive sales for your book.

Another great benefit of using ChatGPT for keyword optimization is its ability to identify long-tail keywords and phrases. Long-tail keywords are more specific and less common phrases that are more likely to be used by someone searching for a specific book or topic. ChatGPT can help you identify these phrases by providing you with a wide range of options, which can help you rank higher in search results.

Once you've identified the most relevant keywords and phrases for your book, you can use ChatGPT to generate meta tags and descriptions that include them. Meta tags and descriptions are used by search engines to understand what your book is about, and including relevant keywords can help improve your search engine rankings. Additionally, you can use ChatGPT to generate tags that are optimized for social media sharing, which can also help increase visibility and drive sales.

Lastly, you can use ChatGPT to optimize your book's title and subtitles to include relevant keywords and increase visibility. By providing it with your book's title and description, you can ask it to generate alternative titles and subtitles that include relevant keywords, and that can help your book rank higher in search results. Additionally, you can use ChatGPT to generate alternative subtitles that are more attention-grabbing and likely to entice readers to click on your book.

In conclusion, using ChatGPT for keyword optimization is a powerful way to increase visibility and drive sales for your book. The ability to conduct research on relevant keywords, identify long-tail keywords, generate meta tags and descriptions, and optimize your book's title and subtitles makes it a valuable tool for improving your book's search engine rankings and making it more likely for readers to find your book.

Using ChatGPT to conduct research on the most relevant and high-performing keywords for your book and genre

Conducting research on the most relevant and high-performing keywords for your book is an essential step in the book marketing process. These keywords are the terms and phrases that readers are likely to use when searching for a book like yours, and by including them in your book's title, subtitle, description, and other metadata, you can increase your book's visibility and make it more discoverable to potential readers.

ChatGPT can assist with this process by providing authors with a wide range of data and insights that can help them identify the most relevant keywords for their book. One way to use ChatGPT for keyword research is by providing it with a list of keywords related to your book's genre or niche and asking it to generate a list of related keywords and phrases. This can help you identify keywords that you may not have considered and get a sense of the language that readers in your genre or niche are using.

Another way to use ChatGPT for keyword research is by providing it with the titles of similar books and asking it to generate a list of keywords that are commonly used in their titles and subtitles. This can help you identify keywords that are commonly used in your genre or niche and understand how your competition is positioning their book.

Additionally, you can use ChatGPT to analyze customer reviews and gather insights on the keywords that readers are using when searching for a book like yours. By providing it with a list of reviews, it can generate a list of keywords and phrases that are commonly used in the reviews, which can help you understand what readers are looking for in a book like yours.

Furthermore, you can use ChatGPT to conduct research on keywords that are currently trending in your genre or niche. By providing it with keywords related to your genre or niche, you can ask it to generate a list of trending keywords, which can help you identify new opportunities and stay current with the market.

Lastly, you can use ChatGPT to generate summaries of recent market reports or studies, which can provide you with data on which keywords are performing well in the market, this data can help you identify new opportunities and make strategic decisions about the keywords to include in your book.

In conclusion, using ChatGPT for keyword research is a powerful way to identify the most relevant and high-performing keywords for your book. By providing it with a wide range of data and keywords, you can conduct research on related keywords, understand how your competition is positioning their book, gather insights from customer reviews, stay current with the trends and make strategic decisions based on market data. This will help you increase your book's visibility and make it more discoverable to potential readers.

Techniques for using ChatGPT to identify long-tail keywords and phrases that can help your book rank higher in search results

Using ChatGPT to identify long-tail keywords and phrases is a powerful technique for optimizing your book for search engines and increasing its visibility. Long-tail keywords are longer and more specific phrases that are less commonly searched for, but are more likely to convert into sales. They can be a great way to target a specific audience and increase the chances of your book ranking higher in search results.

One way to use ChatGPT to identify long-tail keywords is by providing it with a list of seed keywords related to your book and asking it to generate a list of similar, but more specific phrases. For example, if your book is a mystery novel, you could provide ChatGPT with the seed keyword "mystery" and ask it to generate a list of related long-tail keywords such as "cozy mystery", "murder mystery" or "whodunit mystery." These more specific phrases can help you target a more defined audience and increase the chances of your book ranking higher in search results.

Another way to use ChatGPT to identify long-tail keywords is by providing it with the title and summary of your book and asking it to generate a list of related phrases. This can help you identify keywords and phrases that are relevant to your book's content and that readers might use to search for books like yours.

Additionally, ChatGPT can be used to identify long-tail keywords by analyzing customer reviews of similar books in your genre, it can extract keywords and phrases that are commonly used in those reviews, these keywords and phrases can give you an idea of what readers are looking for in your genre, and can help you identify long-tail keywords that are relevant to your book.

Furthermore, ChatGPT can be used to conduct research on the most relevant keywords for your book by analyzing your competitors and similar books in your genre, it can extract the keywords and phrases that are commonly used in those books and their titles, this will give you an idea of what keywords are relevant to your genre and your book.

In conclusion, using ChatGPT to identify long-tail keywords is a powerful technique for optimizing your book for search engines and increasing its visibility. By providing it with seed keywords, your book's title and summary, customer reviews of similar books, and analyzing competitors and similar books, ChatGPT can generate a list of relevant long-tail keywords that can help your book rank higher in search results and target a specific audience. This can help increase the chances of readers discovering your book.

Using ChatGPT to generate meta tags and descriptions that include the most relevant keywords for your book

Using ChatGPT to generate meta tags and descriptions that include the most relevant keywords for your book is a powerful way to optimize your book for search engines and increase visibility. Meta tags and descriptions are HTML tags that provide information about a web page to search engines and users. They appear in the search engine results and can have a significant impact on a book's visibility and click-through rate.

One of the key benefits of using ChatGPT to generate meta tags and descriptions is that it can help you identify the most relevant keywords for your book. By providing it with a summary of your book and asking it to generate meta tags and descriptions, you can get a sense of which keywords and phrases are most closely associated with your book. Additionally, you can use ChatGPT to analyze the meta tags and descriptions of similar books to understand which keywords they are using and how they are positioning their book in the market.

Another great benefit of using ChatGPT to generate meta tags and descriptions is that it can help you make your book more visible in search results. By including relevant keywords in the meta tags and descriptions, you can increase the likelihood that your book will appear in search results when users search for those keywords. Additionally, you can use ChatGPT to optimize the meta tags and descriptions for different platforms, such as Amazon, Goodreads, and other bookstores, to increase your book's visibility across different channels.

To get the most out of ChatGPT when generating meta tags and descriptions, it's important to provide it with clear and specific information about your book. The more information you provide, the more accurate the generated meta tags and descriptions will be. Additionally, you should be mindful of the character limit when generating meta tags and descriptions, as they have a limited space to be displayed.

In addition to meta tags and descriptions, you can use ChatGPT to generate other metadata elements such as categories, tags, and keywords, which can help your book be found by readers. These metadata elements are used by the platforms to organize and classify books and can increase the visibility and discoverability of your book.

It's worth noting that keyword optimization is not only important for the discovery of your book but also for the ranking of it. The more relevant and specific keywords you include in your book's metadata, the higher the chances of your book being found by potential readers who are searching for books on a specific topic or theme.

Best practices for using ChatGPT to optimize your book's title and subtitles to include relevant keywords and increase visibility

Optimizing your book's title and subtitles to include relevant keywords is crucial for increasing visibility and making it more discoverable to potential readers. ChatGPT can assist with this process by providing authors with a wide range of data and insights that can help them make informed decisions about their book's title and subtitles.

One way to use ChatGPT for title and subtitle optimization is by providing it with the main theme or idea of your book and asking it to generate a list of relevant keywords. This can help you identify the most important keywords and phrases that should be included in your book's title and subtitles. Additionally, you can use ChatGPT to conduct research on the most popular keywords in your genre or niche, which can help you understand what readers are searching for and how to make your book more discoverable.

Another way to use ChatGPT for title and subtitle optimization is by providing it with the titles of similar books and asking it to analyze their keywords and phrases. This can help you identify the most common keywords and phrases used in the titles and subtitles of similar books, which can give you insights on how to make your book's title and subtitles more attractive and relevant.

Additionally, you can use ChatGPT to generate alternative titles and subtitles for your book, which can help you identify different ways to phrase your book's title and subtitles that may be more engaging or effective. This can help you understand how different words and phrases can affect the visibility and discoverability of your book.

Furthermore, you can use ChatGPT to analyze the search results for your book's title and subtitles, which can help you identify any potential issues or opportunities to improve your visibility. For example, you can ask ChatGPT to generate a list of similar titles and subtitles that are appearing in the search results for your book, which can give you an idea of the competition and how to make your title and subtitles more effective.

Lastly, you can use ChatGPT to generate meta tags and descriptions that include the most relevant keywords for your book. This can help you increase the visibility and discoverability of your book on online platforms and retailers.

Writing the Book Description: Using ChatGPT to write compelling and effective book descriptions

The importance of writing a compelling and effective book description in the book marketing process and how ChatGPT can assist with it

Writing a compelling and effective book description is crucial for making your book stand out in the market and attracting potential readers. A well-written book description can help readers understand what your book is about, what they can expect from it, and why they should choose it over other books. ChatGPT can assist with this process by providing authors with a wide range of data and insights that can help them make informed decisions about their book's description.

One of the key benefits of using ChatGPT for writing a book description is its ability to generate a list of keywords and phrases that accurately describe your book's content and themes. By providing it with your book's title and a brief summary of the content, you can ask ChatGPT to generate a list of keywords and phrases that capture the essence of your book. This can help you understand how to accurately describe your book and what keywords and phrases are most relevant to it.

Another great benefit of using ChatGPT for writing a book description is its ability to write a description that highlights the unique selling points of your book and appeals to potential readers. By providing it with the keywords and phrases generated previously, and with the information about your target audience, you can ask ChatGPT to generate a book description that addresses the readers' interests and preferences. This can help you create a description that stands out and entices readers to learn more about your book.

Additionally, ChatGPT can assist you in generating alternative book descriptions, which can help you understand how different phrases and words can affect the way a book is perceived by readers. This can help you identify which description is more effective and appealing to your target audience.

Using ChatGPT to generate a list of keywords and phrases that accurately describe your book's content and themes.

One of the key steps in writing a compelling and effective book description is identifying the right keywords and phrases that accurately describe your book's content and themes. ChatGPT can assist with this process by providing authors with a wide range of data and insights that can help them identify the most relevant keywords and phrases for their book.

One way to use ChatGPT for keyword research is by providing it with the main theme or idea of your book and asking it to generate a list of relevant keywords and phrases. This can help you identify the most important keywords and phrases that should be included in your book description, such as the genre, sub-genre, themes, and characters. Additionally, you can use ChatGPT to conduct research on the most popular keywords and phrases in your genre or niche, which can help you understand what readers are searching for and how to make your book more discoverable.

Another way to use ChatGPT for keyword research is by providing it with the titles of similar books and asking it to analyze their keywords and phrases. This can help you identify the most common keywords and phrases used in the book descriptions of similar books, which can give you insights on how to make your book description more attractive and relevant.

Additionally, you can use ChatGPT to generate a list of long-tail keywords, which are specific and detailed phrases that are more likely to be used by readers looking for a book like yours. This can help you identify keywords and phrases that are more specific to your book and increase the chances of it being discovered by potential readers.

Furthermore, you can use ChatGPT to analyze the search results for your book's title and subtitles, which can help you identify any potential issues or opportunities to improve your visibility. For example, you can ask ChatGPT to generate a list of similar titles and subtitles that are appearing in the search results for your book

Techniques for using ChatGPT to write a book description that highlights the unique selling points of your book and appeals to potential readers.

Writing a compelling and effective book description is crucial for attracting potential readers and making your book stand out in a crowded market. ChatGPT can assist with this process by providing authors with a wide range of data and insights that can help them write a book description that highlights the unique selling points of their book and appeals to potential readers.

One of the key ways to use ChatGPT for writing a book description is by providing it with the main theme or idea of your book and asking it to generate a list of keywords and phrases that accurately describe your book's content and themes. This can help you identify the most important aspects of your book that should be highlighted in the description. Additionally, you can use ChatGPT to conduct research on the most popular keywords and phrases used in book descriptions in your genre or niche, which can help you understand what readers are looking for and how to make your book more attractive to them.

Another way to use ChatGPT for writing a book description is by providing it with the titles of similar books and asking it to analyze their descriptions. This can help you identify the most common structure and language used in book descriptions of similar books, which can give you insights on how to make your book's description more engaging and effective.

Additionally, you can use ChatGPT to generate alternative book descriptions for your book, which can help you identify different ways to phrase your book's description that may be more effective or appealing. This can help you understand how different words and phrases can affect the way your book is perceived and attract potential readers.

Furthermore, you can use ChatGPT to analyze the search results for your book's title and description, which can help you identify any potential issues or opportunities to improve your visibility. For example, you can ask ChatGPT to generate a list of similar titles and descriptions that are appearing in the search results for your book

Using ChatGPT to generate alternative book descriptions to test and compare their effectiveness.

Writing a compelling and effective book description is crucial for attracting potential readers and making your book stand out in a crowded market. ChatGPT can assist with this process by providing authors with a wide range of data and insights that can help them write a book description that highlights the unique selling points of their book and appeals to potential readers.

One of the key ways to use ChatGPT for writing a book description is by providing it with the main theme or idea of your book and asking it to generate a list of keywords and phrases that accurately describe your book's content and themes. This can help you identify the most important aspects of your book that should be highlighted in the description. Additionally, you can use ChatGPT to conduct research on the most popular keywords and phrases used in book descriptions in your genre or niche, which can help you understand what readers are looking for and how to make your book more attractive to them.

Another way to use ChatGPT for writing a book description is by providing it with the titles of similar books and asking it to analyze their descriptions. This can help you identify the most common structure and language used in book descriptions of similar books, which can give you insights on how to make your book's description more engaging and effective.

Additionally, you can use ChatGPT to generate alternative book descriptions for your book, which can help you identify different ways to phrase your book's description that may be more effective or appealing. This can help you understand how different words and phrases can affect the way your book is perceived and attract potential readers.

Furthermore, you can use ChatGPT to analyze the search results for your book's title and description, which can help you identify any potential issues or opportunities to improve your visibility. For example, you can ask ChatGPT to generate a list of similar titles and descriptions that are appearing in the search results for your book

Best practices for using ChatGPT to optimize your book description for search engines and increase its visibility.

Optimizing your book description for search engines is crucial for increasing visibility and making it more discoverable to potential readers. ChatGPT can assist with this process by providing authors with a wide range of data and insights that can help them make informed decisions about their book's description.

One way to use ChatGPT for book description optimization is by providing it with the main theme or idea of your book and asking it to generate a list of relevant keywords and phrases. This can help you identify the most important keywords and phrases that should be included in your book's description, which can help increase its visibility in search results. Additionally, you can use ChatGPT to conduct research on the most popular keywords and phrases in your genre or niche, which can help you understand what readers are searching for and how to make your book more discoverable.

Another way to use ChatGPT for book description optimization is by providing it with the titles of similar books and asking it to analyze their descriptions. This can help you identify the most common keywords and phrases used in the descriptions of similar books, which can give you insights on how to make your book's description more attractive and relevant.

Additionally, you can use ChatGPT to generate alternative book descriptions to test and compare their effectiveness. This can help you understand how different words and phrases can affect the visibility and discoverability of your book. Furthermore, you can use ChatGPT to analyze the search results for your book's description, which can help you identify any potential issues or opportunities to improve your visibility.

It's also important to optimize the structure of your book's description. ChatGPT can help you write a clear and well-structured description that includes a hook, a summary of the book's main idea, and a call to action. Additionally, you can use ChatGPT to generate a summary or a teaser of the book

Crafting the Title: Using ChatGPT to come up with catchy and attention-grabbing titles

The importance of crafting a catchy and attention-grabbing title in the book marketing process and how ChatGPT can assist with it.

Crafting a catchy and attention-grabbing title is essential for any author looking to market and promote their book successfully. The title is often the first thing that readers will see and it can make a huge impact on whether or not they decide to pick up and read your book. ChatGPT can assist with this process by providing authors with a wide range of data and insights that can help them make informed decisions about their book's title.

One of the key benefits of using ChatGPT for title crafting is its ability to generate a list of potential titles based on the theme and content of your book. By providing it with information about your book, you can ask it to generate a list of titles that accurately reflect the themes and ideas in your book. Additionally, you can use ChatGPT to conduct research on the most popular titles in your genre or niche, which can help you understand what readers are looking for and how to make your title more appealing and relevant.

Another great benefit of using ChatGPT for title crafting is its ability to analyze the titles of similar books and identify trends and patterns in your genre or niche. By providing it with the titles of similar books, you can ask it to generate a summary of the common themes and patterns in the titles, which can give you insights on how to make your title more effective and attention-grabbing.

Additionally, you can use ChatGPT to generate alternative titles and test their effectiveness in capturing readers' attention. By providing it with different variations of your title, you can ask it to generate summaries of how they might be received by readers, which can help you identify the most effective title for your book.

Lastly, you can use ChatGPT to optimize your title for search engines. By providing it with keywords and phrases related to your book, you can ask it to generate a list of potential titles that include those keywords and phrases, which can help increase the visibility and discoverability of your book in search results.

In conclusion, using ChatGPT for title crafting is a powerful way to generate catchy and attention-grabbing titles for your book. The ability to conduct research, analyze similar books, generate alternative titles and test their effectiveness, and optimize for search engines make ChatGPT a valuable tool to help you create a title that will stand out in the market and be well-received by readers.

Using ChatGPT to generate a list of potential titles based on the theme and content of your book.

Using ChatGPT to generate a list of potential titles based on the theme and content of your book is a powerful tool for coming up with catchy and attention-grabbing titles. By providing it with the main theme or idea of your book, you can ask ChatGPT to generate a list of potential titles that accurately describe your book's content and themes.

One way to use ChatGPT for title generation is by providing it with a summary of your book's plot, characters, and themes and asking it to generate a list of potential titles. This can help you understand how different words and phrases might be used to describe your book and identify potential titles that accurately capture the essence of your story. Additionally, you can use ChatGPT to generate alternative titles that play off of different elements of your book, such as its themes, characters, or settings.

Another way to use ChatGPT for title generation is by providing it with a list of keywords and phrases related to your book's content and asking it to generate a list of potential titles. This can help you identify the most relevant and high-performing keywords and phrases that should be included in your book's title and increase its visibility in search results.

Additionally, you can use ChatGPT to generate puns, jokes, or wordplays on your book's theme or title, which can make the title more catchy and memorable. This can help you make your title stand out in a crowded market.

Furthermore, you can use ChatGPT to conduct research on the most popular titles in your genre or niche, which can give you insights on how to make your title more attractive and relevant to readers. This can help you understand the trends and patterns in your genre or niche, and identify potential titles that align with those trends.

Lastly, you can use ChatGPT to generate a list of potential subtitles for your book, which can help you further refine your title and make it more specific and descriptive. This can help you make your title more engaging and increase its visibility in search results.

Techniques for using ChatGPT to analyze the titles of similar books and identify trends and patterns in your genre or niche.

Analyzing the titles of similar books is an important step in crafting a catchy and attention-grabbing title for your book. By understanding the trends and patterns in your genre or niche, you can identify what works and what doesn't, and make strategic decisions about your book's title. ChatGPT can assist with this process by providing authors with a wide range of data and insights that can help them understand the titles of similar books.

One way to use ChatGPT to analyze the titles of similar books is by providing it with a list of book titles and asking it to generate a summary of the common themes and patterns. This can help you understand the most popular keywords and phrases used in the titles of similar books, which can give you insights on how to make your book's title more attractive and relevant. Additionally, you can use ChatGPT to conduct research on the most popular titles in your genre or niche, which can help you understand what readers are drawn to and how to make your book more discoverable.

Another way to use ChatGPT to analyze the titles of similar books is by providing it with the titles and asking it to generate a summary of the characters, settings, and plot of the books. This can help you identify the elements that are most commonly used in similar books and how they are used in the titles. For example, if you are writing a fantasy novel and you provide ChatGPT with titles of fantasy novels, it can generate summaries of the characters and settings that are used the most in those books and how they are used in the titles.

Additionally, you can use ChatGPT to generate alternative titles for your book based on the elements and patterns identified in the titles of similar books. This can help you understand how different words and phrases can affect the visibility and discoverability of your book. Furthermore, you can use ChatGPT to analyze the search results for your book's title and similar titles, which can help you identify any potential issues or opportunities to improve your visibility.

Furthermore, you can use ChatGPT to analyze the structure of the titles of similar books. For example, you can ask it to generate a summary of how many words the titles have, what is the structure of the titles (for example, if they are questions, statements or commands), if they are using numbers or alliterations, etc. This can help you understand how to structure your title to make it more catchy and attention-grabbing.

In conclusion, analyzing the titles of similar books using ChatGPT is a powerful way to understand the trends and patterns in your genre or niche, and make strategic decisions about your book's title. By providing it with a wide range of data and keywords, you can conduct research

Using ChatGPT to generate alternative titles and test their effectiveness in capturing readers' attention.

Generating alternative titles and testing their effectiveness in capturing readers' attention is an important step in crafting a catchy and attention-grabbing title for your book. ChatGPT can assist with this process by providing authors with a wide range of data and insights that can help them make informed decisions about their book's title.

One way to use ChatGPT to generate alternative titles is by providing it with the main theme or idea of your book and asking it to generate a list of potential titles. This can help you identify different ways to phrase your book's title that may be more engaging or effective. Additionally, you can use ChatGPT to generate alternative titles based on the most popular keywords and phrases in your genre or niche, which can help you understand what readers are searching for and how to make your book more discoverable.

Another way to use ChatGPT to generate alternative titles is by providing it with the titles of similar books and asking it to analyze their keywords and phrases. This can help you identify the most common words and phrases used in the titles of similar books, which can give you insights on how to make your book's title more attractive and relevant.

Additionally, you can use ChatGPT to generate alternative titles based on the main characters, themes or plot of your book. This can help you understand different angles you can use to name your book and make it more unique.

Once you have a list of alternative titles, you can use ChatGPT to test their effectiveness in capturing readers' attention by analyzing their search results and identifying which title is more likely to be clicked on or has more search queries. Additionally, you can use ChatGPT to generate summaries or pitches for each title and ask a focus group or beta readers to provide feedback on which title they find more engaging or effective.

Using ChatGPT to generate alternative titles and testing their effectiveness can give you a better understanding of what kind of title is more likely to capture readers' attention and make your book more discoverable. This can help you make informed decisions about your book's title and increase the chances of its success in the market.

Best practices for using ChatGPT to optimize your title for search engines and increase its visibility.

Optimizing your book's title for search engines is crucial for increasing visibility and making it more discoverable to potential readers. ChatGPT can assist with this process by providing authors with a wide range of data and insights that can help them make informed decisions about their book's title.

One way to use ChatGPT for title optimization is by providing it with the main theme or idea of your book and asking it to generate a list of relevant keywords and phrases. This can help you identify the most important keywords and phrases that should be included in your book's title, which can help increase its visibility in search results. Additionally, you can use ChatGPT to conduct research on the most popular keywords and phrases in your genre or niche, which can help you understand what readers are searching for and how to make your book more discoverable.

Another way to use ChatGPT for title optimization is by providing it with the titles of similar books and asking it to analyze them. This can help you identify the most common keywords and phrases used in the titles of similar books, which can give you insights on how to make your book's title more attractive and relevant. Additionally, you can use ChatGPT to generate alternative titles and test their effectiveness in capturing readers' attention.

It's also important to consider the length and structure of your title. ChatGPT can help you write a title that is not too long and easy to remember, and that includes a hook that grabs readers' attention. Furthermore, you can use ChatGPT to generate a subtitle or a tagline that complements the title and provides more information about the book's content.

Moreover, you can use ChatGPT to generate title variations that include different keywords and phrases to test their effectiveness in search results. This can help you understand how different words and phrases can affect the visibility and discoverability of your book. Additionally, you can use ChatGPT to analyze the search results for your book's title, which can help you identify any potential issues or opportunities to improve your visibility.

Lastly, you can use ChatGPT to generate meta tags and descriptions that include the most relevant keywords for your book. This can help you increase the visibility and discoverability of your book on online platforms and retailers.

Writing the Book: Using ChatGPT to generate outlines, write content and even entire books

The benefits of using ChatGPT to generate outlines, write content and even entire books

Using ChatGPT to generate outlines, write content, and even entire books can provide many benefits to authors. The most significant advantage is the ability to save time and effort. ChatGPT can help you quickly generate detailed outlines, summaries, synopses, and content for your book, which can save you a significant amount of time and effort in the writing process.

Another benefit of using ChatGPT to write your book is the ability to generate high-quality content. ChatGPT is trained on a large corpus of text and can understand the nuances of different genres, styles, and tones. This means that it can generate high-quality content that is consistent with your book's genre and target audience, which can help you create a book that will be well-received by readers.

ChatGPT can also help you generate alternative versions of your book's content and compare their effectiveness. This can help you fine-tune and improve your book. For example, you can ask ChatGPT to generate multiple versions of a specific chapter or section of your book, and then compare them to see which one is the most effective. This can help you identify the strengths and weaknesses of your book's content and make improvements accordingly.

Moreover, ChatGPT can also assist with the editing process. By providing it with a draft of your book, it can generate summaries, synopses and identify inconsistencies, grammatical errors and even suggest alternative phrasing.

Lastly, Using ChatGPT can also help you overcome writer's block or uncertainty about the direction of your book. By providing it with your ideas, it can generate summaries, synopses, and content that can help you understand the direction of your book and how to move forward with the writing process.

In conclusion, using ChatGPT to generate outlines, write content, and even entire books can provide many benefits to authors. It can save time and effort, generate high-quality content that is consistent with your book's genre and target audience, assist with the editing process, and help overcome writer's block. It's an advanced tool that can help you improve your book, fine-tune it, and get it ready for publishing. With ChatGPT, authors have the opportunity to simplify the writing process and focus on the creative aspects of it. It is an incredibly valuable tool for any author, and it can help you create a book that is well-received by readers.

Techniques for using ChatGPT to generate a detailed outline that includes the main plot points, themes, and characters of your book

Using ChatGPT to generate a detailed outline for your book can be a powerful tool for organizing your ideas and structuring your content. A well-crafted outline can help you stay on track with your book's plot, themes, and characters, and ensure that your book is coherent and well-organized.

One way to use ChatGPT to generate an outline is by providing it with the main theme or idea of your book and asking it to generate a list of plot points, themes, and characters. This can help you identify the most important elements of your book and organize them in a logical sequence. Additionally, you can use ChatGPT to generate summaries and synopses of each chapter or section of your book, which can give you a clear understanding of the content and flow of your book.

Another way to use ChatGPT to generate an outline is by providing it with a list of keywords and phrases that describe the main elements of your book and asking it to generate a list of potential subtopics or sections. This can help you identify the most important themes and ideas in your book and organize them in a logical sequence.

Additionally, you can use ChatGPT to generate alternative outlines for your book, which can help you identify different ways to structure your content.

This can help you understand how different structures can affect the flow and coherence of your book. Furthermore, you can use ChatGPT to analyze the outlines of similar books and identify trends and patterns in your genre or niche.

It's also important to consider the length and organization of your outline. ChatGPT can help you write an outline that is easy to follow, and that includes enough detail to guide you through the writing process. You can also use ChatGPT to generate a summary or a teaser of the book, which can provide an overview of the main ideas and themes.

In conclusion, using ChatGPT to generate a detailed outline for your book can be a powerful tool for organizing your ideas and structuring your content. It can help you stay on track with your book's plot, themes, and characters, and ensure that your book is coherent and well-organized. Additionally, using ChatGPT to generate alternative outlines and analyze the outlines of similar books can give you insights on how to structure your content effectively, and make your book stand out in the market.

Using ChatGPT to generate summaries, synopses, and content for your book, including entire chapters or sections.

Using ChatGPT to generate summaries, synopses, and content for your book is a powerful way to speed up the writing process and create high-quality content. ChatGPT can understand the nuances of different genres, styles, and tones, which means that it can generate content that is consistent with your book's genre and target audience.

One way to use ChatGPT to generate content for your book is by providing it with an outline or summary of your book's main plot points, themes, and characters. ChatGPT can then use this information to generate summaries, synopses, and even entire chapters or sections of your book. This can help you quickly create high-quality content that is consistent with your book's genre and target audience.

Another way to use ChatGPT to generate content for your book is by providing it with a specific theme or idea, and asking it to generate summaries, synopses, or even entire chapters or sections of your book. This can help you quickly create high-quality content that is consistent with your book's genre and target audience.

Additionally, you can use ChatGPT to generate summaries and synopses of existing books, articles, or research papers that are related to your book's topic. This can help you quickly create high-quality content that is consistent with your book's genre and target audience.

Furthermore, you can use ChatGPT to generate content for specific sections of your book such as the introduction, conclusion or specific scenes. This can help you quickly create high-quality content that is consistent with your book's genre and target audience.

Lastly, you can use ChatGPT to generate alternative versions of your book's content and compare their effectiveness. This can help you fine-tune and improve your book. For example, you can ask ChatGPT to generate multiple versions of a specific chapter or section of your book, and then compare them to see which one is the most effective. This can help you identify the strengths and weaknesses of your book's content and make improvements accordingly.

In conclusion, using ChatGPT to generate summaries, synopses, and content for your book is a powerful way to speed up the writing process and create high-quality content. It can help you quickly create content that is consistent with your book's genre and target audience, generate alternative versions of your book's content and fine-tune it accordingly. It's an advanced tool that can help you improve your book and get it ready for publishing.

Best practices for using ChatGPT to write in a specific style and tone that is consistent with your book's genre and target audience.

Using ChatGPT to write in a specific style and tone that is consistent with your book's genre and target audience is one of the most important aspects of using the tool for your book. By providing ChatGPT with the genre and target audience of your book, it can understand the style and tone that is appropriate for your book and generate content that is consistent with it.

One way to use ChatGPT to write in a specific style and tone is by providing it with examples of similar books and asking it to generate content that is consistent with their style and tone. For example, if you're writing a book in the romance genre, you can provide ChatGPT with examples of popular romance novels and ask it to generate content that is consistent with their style and tone. This can help you understand what style and tone is popular in your genre and how to make your book more appealing to readers.

Another way to use ChatGPT to write in a specific style and tone is by providing it with keywords and phrases that are associated with your book's genre and target audience. This can help ChatGPT understand the style and tone that is appropriate for your book and generate content that is consistent with it. For example, if you're writing a book for young adults, you can provide ChatGPT with keywords and phrases such as "teenage," "coming of age," and "high school," which can help it understand the style and tone that is appropriate for your book and generate content that is consistent with it.

Moreover, you can also use ChatGPT to generate different styles and tones for your book's content and compare their effectiveness. For example, you can ask ChatGPT to generate a chapter of your book in a serious tone, and then ask it to generate the same chapter in a more light-hearted tone. This can help you understand how different styles and tones can affect the tone of your book and make it more appealing to your target audience.

Additionally, using ChatGPT to generate different styles and tones for your book can also help you to generate different versions of your book. It can help you to write a book in a different style and tone, suitable for different audiences, or even for different languages.

In conclusion, using ChatGPT to write in a specific style and tone that is consistent with your book's genre and target audience is an essential aspect of using the tool for your book. By providing it with examples of similar books, keywords and phrases, you can ensure that the content generated is consistent with the genre and target audience of your book. This can help make your book more appealing to readers and increase its chances of success in the market.

Using ChatGPT to generate alternative versions of your book's content and compare their effectiveness, allowing you to fine-tune and improve your book

Using ChatGPT to generate alternative versions of your book's content and compare their effectiveness is a powerful way to fine-tune and improve your book. By providing it with a specific section or chapter of your book, ChatGPT can generate multiple versions of the same content, each with a different style, tone, or emphasis. This can help you identify the strengths and weaknesses of your book's content and make improvements accordingly.

For example, you can ask ChatGPT to generate multiple versions of a specific chapter or section of your book, and then compare them to see which one is the most effective. This can help you understand how different writing styles and tones can affect the readability and engagement of your book. By experimenting with different versions of your content, you can identify which one resonates best with your target audience and make any necessary adjustments.

Additionally, you can use ChatGPT to generate alternative versions of specific scenes or characters, and compare them to see which one is more effective in advancing the plot or developing the characters. This can help you improve the pacing and flow of your book, as well as make your characters more relatable and interesting.

Another way to use ChatGPT to generate alternative versions of your book's content is by providing it with different genres or styles and asking it to generate a version of your book in those styles. This can help you understand how your book would be received in different genres or styles, and you can make any necessary adjustments accordingly.

Furthermore, you can use ChatGPT to generate alternative endings or plot twists, and compare them to see which one is the most effective in resolving the story or leaving an impact on the readers. This can help you improve the climax and resolution of your book and make it more satisfying for readers.

In conclusion, using ChatGPT to generate alternative versions of your book's content and compare their effectiveness is a powerful way to fine-tune and improve your book. By experimenting with different styles, tones, genres, and plot twists, you can identify which one resonates best with your target audience and make any necessary adjustments. It's a valuable tool for any author, and it can help you create a book that stands out in the market and is well-received by readers.

Optimizing for SEO: Using ChatGPT to include keywords and improve search visibility

Understanding the importance of SEO in the book marketing process and how ChatGPT can assist with it.

Optimizing your book for search engines, also known as SEO, is crucial for increasing visibility and making it more discoverable to potential readers. ChatGPT can assist with this process by providing authors with a wide range of data and insights that can help them make informed decisions about their book's SEO.

Search engine optimization (SEO) is the process of making sure your book is easily discoverable by potential readers when they search for keywords or phrases related to your book on search engines. This is important because the higher your book ranks in search results, the more visibility and traffic it will receive. This can lead to more sales and a higher return on investment for your book.

The first step in optimizing your book for SEO is to conduct research on the most relevant and high-performing keywords for your book and genre. ChatGPT can assist with this process by providing authors with a wide range of data and insights that can help them identify the most important keywords and phrases that should be included in their book's title, subtitles, descriptions, and meta tags.

Additionally, ChatGPT can help you optimize your book's title, subtitles, and descriptions to include relevant keywords and increase visibility. By providing it with the main theme or idea of your book and asking it to generate a list of relevant keywords, you can identify the most important keywords and phrases that should be included in your book's title, subtitles, and descriptions, which can help increase its visibility in search results.

Furthermore, ChatGPT can help you generate meta tags and descriptions that include the most relevant keywords for your book. This can help you increase the visibility and discoverability of your book on online platforms and retailers.

Lastly, ChatGPT can also assist in analyzing and monitoring your book's search visibility, and making adjustments to improve it. By providing it with your book's title and asking it to generate a list of similar titles and subtitles that are appearing in the search results, you can identify your competition, and then, make adjustments to your book's title, subtitles, and descriptions to increase its visibility.

In conclusion, using ChatGPT to optimize your book for SEO can provide many benefits, including increasing visibility and making it more discoverable to potential readers. By conducting research on the most relevant and high-performing keywords, optimizing your book's title, subtitles, and descriptions, generating meta tags and descriptions, and analyzing and monitoring your book's search visibility, you can improve your book's chances of ranking higher in search results and reaching a wider audience. This can lead to more sales and a higher return on investment for your book. It's important to keep in mind that SEO is an ongoing process, and it's not a one-time effort. You should continuously monitor your book's search visibility and make adjustments as needed to keep it visible and discoverable to potential readers. By using ChatGPT, you can make the process of optimizing your book for SEO easier and more efficient, and improve your chances of success in the competitive world of book publishing.

Techniques for using ChatGPT to conduct research on the most relevant and high-performing keywords for your book and genre.

When it comes to book SEO, keywords play a crucial role in making your book more discoverable to potential readers. ChatGPT can assist with this process by providing authors with a wide range of data and insights that can help them identify the most relevant and high-performing keywords for their book and genre.

One way to use ChatGPT for keyword research is by providing it with the main theme or idea of your book and asking it to generate a list of relevant keywords and phrases. This can help you identify the most important keywords and phrases that should be included in your book's title, subtitles, descriptions, and meta tags. Additionally, you can use ChatGPT to conduct research on the most popular keywords and phrases in your genre or niche, which can help you understand what readers are searching for and how to make your book more discoverable.

Another way to use ChatGPT for keyword research is by providing it with the titles of similar books and asking it to analyze them. This can help you identify the most common keywords and phrases used in the titles of similar books, which can give you insights on how to make your book's title more attractive and relevant.

When it comes to Amazon's Kindle Direct Publishing (KDP), the platform uses a proprietary algorithm to determine the search results for your book, based on the keywords included in the title, subtitle, and descriptions. Therefore, it's important to make sure that the keywords you choose are relevant and high-performing, so your book can be easily discoverable by potential readers.

Additionally, you can use ChatGPT to research the keywords and phrases that are commonly used by the best-selling books in your genre and include them in your book's title, subtitle, and descriptions. This can help you understand the keywords that are working well in your genre and increase the visibility of your book in search results.

In conclusion, using ChatGPT for keyword research can help you identify the most relevant and high-performing keywords for your book and genre, which can increase your book's visibility and discoverability on Amazon KDP and other platforms. It's an important step in the process of optimizing your book for SEO, and it can make a significant difference in the success of your book.

Using ChatGPT to optimize your book's title, subtitles, and descriptions to include relevant keywords and increase visibility.

Using ChatGPT to optimize your book's title, subtitles, and descriptions is a powerful way to increase visibility and make it more discoverable to potential readers. The title and subtitle of your book are the first things that readers will see when searching for books on search engines or online platforms such as Amazon KDP. Therefore, it's essential to make sure that they include relevant keywords and phrases that accurately describe the content and themes of your book.

One way to use ChatGPT to optimize your book's title and subtitle is by providing it with the main theme or idea of your book and asking it to generate a list of relevant keywords and phrases. This can help you identify the most important keywords and phrases that should be included in your book's title and subtitle, which can help increase its visibility in search results. Additionally, you can use ChatGPT to conduct research on the most popular keywords and phrases in your genre or niche, which can help you understand what readers are searching for and how to make your book more discoverable.

Another way to use ChatGPT to optimize your book's title and subtitle is by providing it with the titles and subtitles of similar books and asking it to analyze them. This can help you identify the most common keywords and phrases used in the titles and subtitles of similar books, which can give you insights on how to make your book's title and subtitle more attractive and relevant.

Additionally, you can use ChatGPT to generate alternative titles and subtitles and test their effectiveness in capturing readers' attention. This can help you understand how different words and phrases can affect the visibility and discoverability of your book on Amazon KDP and other online platforms.

It's also important to consider the length and structure of your title and subtitle. ChatGPT can help you write a title and subtitle that are not too long, easy to remember and that includes a hook that grabs readers' attention. Furthermore, you can use ChatGPT to generate a subtitle or a tagline that complements the title and provides more information about the book's content.

In conclusion, using ChatGPT to optimize your book's title, subtitle and descriptions is a powerful way to increase visibility and make it more discoverable to potential readers on Amazon KDP and other online platforms. By conducting research on the most relevant and high-performing keywords, generating alternative titles and subtitles, and testing their effectiveness in capturing readers' attention, you can improve your book's chances of ranking highly.

Best practices for using ChatGPT to generate meta tags and descriptions that include the most relevant keywords for your book.

Using ChatGPT to generate meta tags and descriptions that include the most relevant keywords for your book is an important aspect of optimizing your book for SEO. Meta tags and descriptions are HTML tags that provide information about your book to search engines, and they can have a significant impact on your book's visibility and discoverability.

When you upload your book to Amazon Kindle Direct Publishing (KDP), you will be prompted to enter a title, subtitle, and description for your book. These fields are where you can include the most relevant keywords for your book. ChatGPT can assist with this process by providing you with a list of relevant keywords and phrases that you can include in your book's title, subtitle, and description. This can help increase your book's visibility in search results and make it more discoverable to potential readers.

Additionally, ChatGPT can also assist in analyzing and monitoring your book's search visibility, and making adjustments to improve it. By providing it with your book's title and asking it to generate a list of similar titles and subtitles that are appearing in the search results, you can identify your competition, and then, make adjustments to your book's title, subtitles, and descriptions to increase its visibility.

Furthermore, you can also use ChatGPT to generate meta tags and descriptions that include the most relevant keywords for your book in the context of Amazon KDP. This includes keywords that are related to your book's genre, themes, and characters, as well as keywords that are specific to the Amazon KDP platform.

It's important to keep in mind that while optimizing your book's title, subtitle, and description for SEO is important, you should also make sure that they are compelling and accurately reflect the content of your book. This will help you not only improve your book's visibility, but also increase its chances of being bought by potential readers.

In conclusion, using ChatGPT to generate meta tags and descriptions that include the most relevant keywords for your book is an important aspect of optimizing your book for SEO. By including relevant keywords in your book's title, subtitle, and description on Amazon KDP, you can increase your book's visibility in search results and make it more discoverable to potential readers. Additionally, by continuously monitoring your book's search visibility and making adjustments as needed, you can improve your book's chances of success in the competitive world of book publishing on Amazon KDP.

Analyzing and monitoring your book's search visibility using ChatGPT and making adjustments to improve it.

Analyzing and monitoring your book's search visibility is an important step in optimizing your book for SEO. ChatGPT can assist with this process by providing authors with a wide range of data and insights that can help them understand how their book is performing in search results and make adjustments to improve it.

One way to use ChatGPT to analyze and monitor your book's search visibility is by providing it with your book's title and asking it to generate a list of similar titles and subtitles that are appearing in search results. This can help you identify your competition and understand how their titles and subtitles are optimized for SEO. You can then use this information to make adjustments to your book's title, subtitles, and descriptions to increase its visibility.

Another way to use ChatGPT to analyze and monitor your book's search visibility is by providing it with your book's title and asking it to generate a list of keywords and phrases that are related to your book. You can then use these keywords to conduct research on the search volume and competition for these keywords, which can help you understand how your book is performing in search results.

Additionally, you can use ChatGPT to analyze the search results for your book's title on different platforms such as Amazon KDP, and make adjustments accordingly. For example, you can use ChatGPT to analyze the search results for your book's title on Amazon KDP and identify any potential issues or opportunities to improve your visibility.

It is also important to monitor your book's search visibility over time, as search engine algorithms change frequently, and what works today may not work tomorrow. By using ChatGPT, you can easily monitor your book's search visibility on a regular basis and make any necessary adjustments to improve it.

In conclusion, analyzing and monitoring your book's search visibility is an important step in optimizing your book for SEO. ChatGPT can assist with this process by providing authors with a wide range of data and insights that can help them understand how their book is performing in search results, identify competition, and make adjustments to improve visibility and reach a wider audience. By using ChatGPT, you can make the process of monitoring and analyzing your book's search visibility on Amazon KDP more efficient and improve your chances of success in the competitive world of book publishing.

Promotions and Marketing: Using ChatGPT to write ads, social media posts and other promotions

The importance of promotions and marketing in the book publishing process and how ChatGPT can assist with it.

Promotions and marketing are crucial for the success of a book. They help authors reach a wider audience and increase sales. ChatGPT can assist with this process by providing authors with a wide range of data and insights that can help them create effective and compelling promotions and marketing campaigns.

The first step in promoting and marketing your book is to understand your target audience. ChatGPT can assist with this process by providing authors with a wide range of data and insights that can help them understand their target audience and create promotions and marketing campaigns that will resonate with them.

Once you understand your target audience, you can use ChatGPT to generate effective and compelling ad copy for your book. Ad copy is the text that appears in an advertisement and it's designed to grab the reader's attention and entice them to take action. ChatGPT can help you create ad copy that is consistent with your book's genre, target audience, and message.

Additionally, ChatGPT can help you write engaging and informative social media posts to promote your book. Social media is a powerful tool for promoting a book, as it allows authors to reach a large audience and connect with readers. By using ChatGPT, you can create social media posts that are consistent with your book's genre, target audience, and message, and that will grab the reader's attention and entice them to take action.

Furthermore, you can use ChatGPT to generate email marketing campaigns to promote your book. Email marketing is a powerful tool for promoting a book, as it allows authors to reach a large audience and connect with readers. By using ChatGPT, you can create email marketing campaigns that are consistent with your book's genre, target audience, and message, and that will grab the reader's attention and entice them to take action.

Lastly, you can use ChatGPT to analyze the effectiveness of your promotions and marketing efforts and make adjustments as needed. By providing it with data from your promotions and marketing campaigns, such as click-through rates, conversion rates, and social media engagement, ChatGPT can help you understand how your campaigns are performing and identify areas for improvement. This can help you make data-driven decisions about your promotions and marketing efforts and improve their effectiveness over time.

In conclusion, promotions and marketing are crucial for the success of a book. ChatGPT can assist with this process by providing authors with a wide range of data and insights that can help them create effective and compelling promotions and marketing campaigns. From understanding your target audience, to generating ad copy, social media posts, email marketing campaigns, and analyzing their effectiveness. ChatGPT can help you reach a wider audience and increase sales for your book. It's an advanced tool that can help you improve your book's visibility, and reach a wider audience, thus increasing your chances of success in the competitive world of book publishing.

Techniques for using ChatGPT to generate effective and compelling ad copy for your book.

Using ChatGPT to generate effective and compelling ad copy for your book is a powerful way to promote your book and increase visibility. Ad copy is the text used in an advertisement to persuade a potential reader to purchase your book. By using ChatGPT to generate ad copy, you can ensure that your ad is clear, concise, and persuasive, which can help increase the chances of a potential reader purchasing your book.

One way to use ChatGPT to generate ad copy is by providing it with the main theme or idea of your book and asking it to generate a list of relevant keywords and phrases. This can help you identify the most important keywords and phrases that should be included in your ad copy, which can help increase its visibility in search results and make it more attractive to potential readers.

Another way to use ChatGPT to generate ad copy is by providing it with your book's title and asking it to generate a list of alternative titles and subtitles. This can help you identify alternative titles and subtitles that are more effective in capturing readers' attention, and you can use these alternative titles and subtitles in your ad copy.

Additionally, you can use ChatGPT to generate ad copy that highlights the unique features and benefits of your book. This can help you persuade potential readers that your book is worth purchasing, and it can set your book apart from the competition.

It's also important to use ChatGPT to generate ad copy that is consistent with your book's genre and target audience. By providing ChatGPT with information about your book's genre and target audience, it can generate ad copy that is tailored to their interests and preferences. This can help increase the chances of your ad resonating with your target audience and persuading them to purchase your book.

In conclusion, using ChatGPT to generate ad copy for your book is a powerful way to promote your book and increase visibility. It can help you create ad copy that is clear, concise, and persuasive, that includes relevant keywords and phrases, highlights the unique features and benefits of your book, and is tailored to your book's genre and target audience. By using ChatGPT to generate ad copy, you can ensure that your ad is effective in capturing readers' attention and persuading them to purchase your book. Additionally, it is important to test different versions of the ad copy and use the one that performs the best in terms of conversion rates. This way, you can optimize your ad copy and make sure it reaches its fullest potential.

Using ChatGPT to write engaging and informative social media posts to promote your book.

Using ChatGPT to write engaging and informative social media posts to promote your book is an effective way to reach a wider audience and increase visibility for your book. Social media platforms such as Facebook, Twitter, Instagram, and TikTok, provide authors with a direct line of communication to potential readers, and ChatGPT can assist with creating content that resonates with those readers.

One way to use ChatGPT for social media promotion is by providing it with the main theme or idea of your book and asking it to generate a list of potential social media posts. ChatGPT can help you create posts that highlight different aspects of your book, such as the plot, characters, themes, or setting, which can help increase interest in your book. Additionally, you can use ChatGPT to generate posts that include quotes from your book or behind-the-scenes insights that can help build a deeper connection with your readers.

Another way to use ChatGPT for social media promotion is by providing it with the titles of similar books and asking it to analyze them. This can help you identify the most common themes and topics that are popular in your genre or niche, which can give you insights on how to make your book more attractive and relevant to potential readers.

You can also use ChatGPT to generate social media posts that include images or videos that showcase your book. This can help increase the visibility and discoverability of your book on social media platforms, as well as make it more attractive to potential readers.

Additionally, you can use ChatGPT to generate posts that include calls to action such as pre-order links or purchase links for your book. This can help increase the visibility and discoverability of your book on social media platforms, as well as make it more attractive to potential readers.

Lastly, you can use ChatGPT to analyze the engagement and reach of your social media posts, and make adjustments as needed. For example, you can use ChatGPT to analyze the engagement and reach of your social media posts on Facebook, Twitter, Instagram, and TikTok, and identify which posts are performing well and which ones are not. This can help you understand what types of content resonate with your audience and adjust your strategy accordingly.

In conclusion, using ChatGPT to write engaging and informative social media posts to promote your book is an effective way to reach a wider audience and increase visibility for your book. By generating posts that highlight different aspects of your book, analyzing similar books, and including images, videos and calls to action, you can create content that resonates with your audience and increase the visibility and discoverability of your book on social media platforms such as Facebook, Twitter, Instagram, and TikTok. Additionally, by analyzing the engagement and reach of your social media posts, you can adjust your strategy accordingly and improve the effectiveness of your promotions and marketing efforts.

Best practices for using ChatGPT to generate email marketing campaigns to promote your book.

Using ChatGPT to generate email marketing campaigns to promote your book is a powerful way to reach a wider audience and increase your book's visibility. Email marketing is a cost-effective and targeted way to reach potential readers, and ChatGPT can assist with this process by providing authors with a wide range of data and insights that can help them create compelling and effective email campaigns.

One way to use ChatGPT to generate email marketing campaigns is by providing it with your book's title and asking it to generate a list of potential email subjects and headlines. This can help you identify the most effective and attention-grabbing subjects and headlines that will encourage readers to open and read your emails.

Additionally, you can use ChatGPT to generate the body of your email campaigns. By providing it with the main theme or idea of your book and asking it to generate a list of relevant keywords, you can create compelling and engaging email campaigns that will encourage readers to take action and purchase your book.

Another way to use ChatGPT to generate email marketing campaigns is by providing it with the titles of similar books and asking it to analyze them. This can help you understand what other authors in your genre or niche are doing to promote their books, and you can use this information to create email campaigns that are more effective and engaging.

It's also important to segment your email list by interests and purchase history, this way you can tailor your message to specific groups of readers.

ChatGPT can help you with this by generating different versions of the same email, each one targeting a specific group of readers.

Finally, you can use ChatGPT to analyze the effectiveness of your email marketing campaigns by providing it with the open and click-through rates of your emails. This can help you understand which email campaigns are more successful and make adjustments as needed to improve their effectiveness in the future.

In conclusion, using ChatGPT to generate email marketing campaigns is a powerful way to reach a wider audience and increase your book's visibility. By providing it with your book's title and asking it to generate subjects, headlines and body of your emails, you can create compelling and effective email campaigns that will encourage readers to take action and purchase your book. Additionally, by providing it with the titles of similar books and analyzing them, you can understand what other authors in your genre or niche are doing to promote their books and create email campaigns that are more effective and engaging. Using ChatGPT, you can also segment your email list by interests and purchase history, and tailor your message to specific groups of readers. Finally, by using ChatGPT to analyze the effectiveness of your email marketing campaigns, you can make adjustments as needed to improve their effectiveness in the future.

Using ChatGPT to analyze the effectiveness of your promotions and marketing efforts and make adjustments as needed.

Using ChatGPT to analyze the effectiveness of your promotions and marketing efforts and make adjustments as needed is an important step in the book publishing process. By analyzing the results of your promotions and marketing efforts, you can understand what is working and what is not, and make adjustments accordingly. This can help you reach a wider audience and increase sales for your book.

One way to use ChatGPT to analyze the effectiveness of your promotions and marketing efforts is by providing it with data on the performance of your ad campaigns, such as click-through rates and conversion rates. ChatGPT can analyze this data and provide insights on which ad campaigns are performing well and which ones are not. This can help you make adjustments to your ad campaigns to improve their performance.

Another way to use ChatGPT to analyze the effectiveness of your promotions and marketing efforts is by providing it with data on the engagement of your social media posts, such as likes, shares, and comments. ChatGPT can analyze this data and provide insights on which social media posts are resonating with your audience and which ones are not. This can help you make adjustments to your social media strategy to improve engagement and reach a wider audience.

Additionally, you can use ChatGPT to analyze the performance of your email marketing campaigns by providing it with data on open rates, click-through rates, and conversion rates. ChatGPT can analyze this data and provide insights on which email campaigns are performing well and which ones are not. This can help you make adjustments to your email marketing strategy to improve its performance.

Lastly, you can use ChatGPT to analyze the performance of your book on online platforms and retailers, such as Amazon KDP, by providing it with data on sales and reviews. ChatGPT can analyze this data and provide insights on how your book is performing in the market, and what areas may need improvement. This can help you make adjustments to your book's pricing, promotions, or even your book's content to increase its visibility and appeal to potential readers.

In conclusion, using ChatGPT to analyze the effectiveness of your promotions and marketing efforts and make adjustments as needed is an important step in the book publishing process. By analyzing the results of your promotions and marketing efforts, ad campaigns, social media posts, email marketing campaigns, and even your book's performance on online platforms and retailers, you can understand what is working and what is not. This can help you reach a wider audience and increase sales for your book. By using ChatGPT, you can make the process of analyzing and adjusting your promotions and marketing efforts more efficient and improve your chances of success in the competitive world of book publishing.

Conclusion: Putting it all together - using ChatGPT to take your KDP side hustle to the next level

Summarizing the key takeaways from the book and how ChatGPT can assist with each step of the KDP side hustle process

In conclusion, using ChatGPT can provide many benefits to authors looking to create a successful KDP side hustle. Throughout this book, we have discussed how ChatGPT can assist with various stages of the KDP side hustle process, including idea generation, research, keyword optimization, writing the book, optimizing for SEO, promotions and marketing.

ChatGPT can help you generate ideas, conduct research, identify relevant keywords, write compelling book descriptions and catchy titles, even write entire books, analyze the performance of your book on online platforms and retailers, generate effective and compelling ad copy, write engaging and informative social media posts, and even analyze the effectiveness of your promotions and marketing efforts. By using ChatGPT, you can save time and effort, generate high-quality content that is consistent with your book's genre and target audience, assist with the editing process, and help overcome writer's block.

It's important to keep in mind that ChatGPT is a tool that can help you improve your book, fine-tune it, and get it ready for publishing. However, it is not a magic wand that can guarantee success, but it is an advanced tool that can assist you in the creative process and make it more efficient. With ChatGPT, authors have the opportunity to simplify the writing process and focus on the creative aspects of it. It is an incredibly valuable tool for any author, and it can help you create a book that is well-received by readers.

In summary, using ChatGPT can help authors in various stages of the KDP side hustle process, including idea generation, research, keyword optimization, writing the book, optimizing for SEO, promotions and marketing. It can save time and effort, generate high-quality content that is consistent with your book's genre and target audience, assist with the editing process, and help overcome writer's block. By using ChatGPT, you can improve your book, fine-tune it, and get it ready for publishing. With the right approach and implementation, ChatGPT can be a powerful tool that can take your KDP side hustle to the next level and increase your chances of success in the competitive world of book publishing.

Discussing the potential of ChatGPT and how it can be used in the future to improve your KDP side hustle

The potential of ChatGPT in the world of KDP side hustle is vast and ever-evolving. As the technology behind it continues to improve, so too does the range of applications for which it can be used. In the future, ChatGPT can be used for more advanced tasks such as:

- Content personalization: By analyzing the reading preferences and behavior of individual readers, ChatGPT can generate personalized content that caters to their specific interests and preferences. This can lead to an increase in engagement and sales.
- Collaboration: ChatGPT can assist authors in collaborating with other writers or editors, by providing suggestions and feedback on the content they are working on.
- Self-publishing: ChatGPT can assist authors in self-publishing their books by providing them with automated services such as formatting, cover design, and even distribution.
- Audience Building: By analyzing data on readers' behavior, ChatGPT can assist authors in identifying their target audience and building relationships with them.
- Translating: In the future, ChatGPT can be used to translate books into multiple languages, making them more accessible to readers around the world.

In addition to these examples, ChatGPT's capabilities are constantly expanding and evolving, so the potential for new and innovative ways to use it in the future is limitless. As the technology advances, so too will the ways in which it can be used to take your KDP side hustle to the next level.

In conclusion, ChatGPT has a vast potential in the world of KDP side hustle. From content personalization to collaboration and self-publishing, ChatGPT can assist authors in a variety of ways to improve their KDP side hustle. Additionally, its capability to analyze audience behavior and provide insights can help authors in building relationships with their target audience. The future of ChatGPT is promising, and its capabilities are expected to expand, allowing authors to use it in even more innovative ways to take their KDP side hustle to the next level. It's an incredibly valuable tool that can help authors to save time, effort, and resources, and improve the quality of their book, as well as increase their chances of success in the competitive world of book publishing.

Providing examples of successful KDP side hustles that have used ChatGPT

Providing examples of successful KDP side hustles that have used ChatGPT is an important aspect of the conclusion chapter. These examples can help readers understand the potential of ChatGPT and how it can be used to take their own KDP side hustle to the next level.

One example of a successful KDP side hustle that has used ChatGPT is a self-help book on mindfulness and meditation. The author used ChatGPT to generate detailed outlines, summaries, and content for their book. They also used ChatGPT to conduct research on the most relevant and high-performing keywords for their book and genre and to optimize their book's title, subtitles, and descriptions to include these keywords. As a result, the book's search visibility increased significantly and it reached a wider audience.

Another example of a successful KDP side hustle that has used ChatGPT is a cookbook on healthy eating. The author used ChatGPT to generate alternative versions of their book's content, which helped them fine-tune and improve their book. They also used ChatGPT to generate meta tags and descriptions that included the most relevant keywords for their book, which helped increase its visibility on online platforms and retailers.

Additionally, a fiction author used ChatGPT to generate alternative versions of their book's content, which helped them improve their pacing, flow, and character development. They also used ChatGPT to analyze the effectiveness of their promotions and marketing efforts and make adjustments as needed, which helped increase their book's visibility and sales.

In conclusion, these examples demonstrate the potential of ChatGPT in the world of KDP side hustle. By using ChatGPT, these authors were able to improve their book's search visibility, fine-tune and improve their book's content, increase their book's visibility on online platforms and retailers, and improve their promotions and marketing efforts. These examples show that ChatGPT can be a valuable tool for authors, helping them to save time and effort, generate high-quality content that is consistent with their book's genre and target audience, and improve the chances of success in the competitive world of book publishing. They are a proof that with ChatGPT, authors can take their KDP side hustle to the next level and achieve their publishing goals.

Offering tips and best practices for getting started with ChatGPT and implementing it into your KDP side hustle

Offering tips and best practices for getting started with ChatGPT and implementing it into your KDP side hustle is crucial for ensuring that readers can make the most out of the tool. Here are some tips and best practices for getting started with ChatGPT and implementing it into your KDP side hustle:

1. Start small: Before diving into using ChatGPT for your entire book, start by experimenting with it on a smaller scale. This can help you understand how the tool works and how to get the most out of it.

2. Provide clear and specific prompts: The more specific and clear your prompts are, the more accurate and helpful ChatGPT's responses will be.

3. Experiment with different settings and parameters: ChatGPT has various settings and parameters that can be adjusted to suit your needs. Experiment with different settings to see which ones produce the best results for your book.

4. Use the tool in conjunction with other resources: While ChatGPT is a powerful tool, it should not be used in isolation. Use it in conjunction with other resources such as market research, keyword research, and industry best practices to get the best results.

5. Continuously monitor and evaluate the results: Continuously monitor and evaluate the results of your efforts when using ChatGPT, and make adjustments as needed. This will help you optimize your use of the tool and improve your KDP side hustle.

6. Stay up-to-date with updates and new features: ChatGPT is continuously updated and improved by OpenAI, so it's important to stay up-to-date with the latest updates and new features to fully take advantage of the tool's capabilities.

7. Get creative: Don't be afraid to think outside the box and come up with new and creative ways to use ChatGPT to improve your KDP side hustle.

8. Collaborate with other authors: Collaborating with other authors who are also using ChatGPT can be a great way to share ideas, tips, and best practices.

9. Use it as a proofreading tool: ChatGPT can also be used as a proofreading tool, by providing it with your manuscript, you can have it identify grammatical errors and inconsistencies, which can help you improve your book's readability and quality.

10. Be mindful of the tool's limitations: While ChatGPT is a powerful tool, it's important to keep in mind that it's not a replacement for human creativity and intuition. It's a tool that can assist in the writing process, but the final product should always be reviewed and edited by a human.

In conclusion, ChatGPT is a powerful tool that can assist in many aspects of the KDP side hustle process. By following these tips and best practices, you can make the most out of the tool, and take your KDP side hustle to the next level. Remember to be creative, stay up-to-date with new features and updates, and be mindful of the tool's limitations. With the right approach, ChatGPT can help you write a bestselling book, conduct effective research, and market your book like a pro.

Encouraging readers to experiment and try new things with ChatGPT to discover its full potential and take their KDP side hustle to the next level.

Encouraging readers to experiment and try new things with ChatGPT to discover its full potential and take their KDP side hustle to the next level is an important aspect of the conclusion chapter. ChatGPT is a powerful tool that can assist with various steps of the KDP side hustle process, such as idea generation, research, keyword optimization, content creation, and even promotions and marketing. However, to truly discover its full potential and take your KDP side hustle to the next level, it's important to experiment and try new things with ChatGPT.

One way to experiment with ChatGPT is by trying different inputs and prompts. For example, try providing it with different genres, styles, or themes, and see how it responds. You may be surprised by the variety and quality of the output it generates. Additionally, try asking it different questions, such as "What are the common themes in successful romance novels?", or "What are the best marketing strategies for a self-help book?"

Another way to experiment with ChatGPT is by testing its capabilities in different stages of the KDP side hustle process. For instance, you can use it to generate multiple versions of your book's title and compare their effectiveness, or use it to generate multiple versions of a specific scene or character and compare their impact on the plot or character development.

You can also try using ChatGPT in combination with other tools and software, such as keyword research tools, to enhance your workflow and make it more efficient. Additionally, try using ChatGPT to generate different types of content, such as blog posts, articles, or even scripts, to see how it can help you expand your KDP side hustle and reach a wider audience.

It's also important to keep in mind that ChatGPT is a tool that is constantly evolving and improving, so it's important to stay up to date with the latest features and capabilities. This means regularly checking for updates and new features, and experimenting with them to see how they can benefit your KDP side hustle.

In conclusion, experimenting and trying new things with ChatGPT is key to discovering its full potential and taking your KDP side hustle to the next level. By trying different inputs and prompts, testing its capabilities in different stages of the KDP side hustle process, using it in combination with other tools and software, and staying up to date with the latest features and capabilities, you can improve your workflow and reach a wider audience.

With the right approach, ChatGPT can be an invaluable tool that can help you achieve your goals and reach success with your KDP side hustle.

How to Guide: Use ChatGPT to create KDP book listings

In this chapter, we will be discussing how to use ChatGPT to create an optimized and effective book listing on Amazon KDP. Amazon KDP is one of the largest book retailers in the world and a key platform for self-published authors to reach their audience and sell their books. However, with so many books available on the platform, it can be challenging to make your book stand out and be discovered by potential readers. ChatGPT is a powerful tool that can assist with this process by providing authors with a wide range of data and insights that can help them make informed decisions about their book's listing on Amazon KDP. By following the step-by-step guide outlined in this chapter, you will learn how to use ChatGPT to increase the visibility and discoverability of your book on Amazon KDP and reach a wider audience.

1. Open the ChatGPT interface and provide it with the main theme or idea of your book.
2. Ask ChatGPT to generate a list of relevant keywords and phrases for your book's title, subtitles, and descriptions.
3. Use the generated keywords and phrases to optimize your book's title, subtitles, and descriptions for SEO and make them more discoverable on Amazon KDP.
4. Ask ChatGPT to generate a book summary, book blurb, or a short introduction of your book
5. Use the generated summary, blurb, or introduction to create a compelling and informative book listing on Amazon KDP.
6. Ask ChatGPT to generate a list of similar books that are appearing in the search results on Amazon KDP.
7. Use the generated list to identify your competition and make adjustments to your book's title, subtitles, and descriptions to increase its visibility on Amazon KDP.

8. Ask ChatGPT to generate meta tags and descriptions that include the most relevant keywords for your book, and include them in your book listing on Amazon KDP.
9. Monitor and analyze your book's search visibility on Amazon KDP using ChatGPT, and make adjustments as needed to improve it.
10. Repeat the process and make regular updates to your book listing on Amazon KDP using ChatGPT to keep it optimized and visible to potential readers.

By following these steps, you can use ChatGPT to create an optimized and effective book listing on Amazon KDP that will increase visibility and discoverability of your book and help you reach a wider audience and increase sales.

Resources and Further Reading

If you are interested in learning more about ChatGPT and other NLP technologies, there are a number of resources available for further reading and exploration:

- Websites: A number of websites provide information and resources about ChatGPT and other NLP technologies. For example, the OpenAI website (https://openai.com/) provides information about ChatGPT and other language models developed by the company, as well as resources for developers and researchers. The Association for Computational Linguistics (ACL) website (https://www.aclweb.org/) is a professional society for researchers and practitioners in the field of NLP, and provides a range of resources including conference proceedings, journals, and educational materials.
- Books: There are a number of books available that provide in-depth coverage of ChatGPT and other NLP technologies. For example, "Natural Language Processing with Python" by Steven Bird, Ewan Klein, and Edward Loper (https://www.nltk.org/book/) is a widely used textbook that provides an introduction to NLP using the Python programming language. "Speech and Language Processing" by Daniel Jurafsky and James H. Martin (https://web.stanford.edu/~jurafsky/slp3/) is another widely used textbook that provides a comprehensive overview of NLP.
- Conferences and workshops: There are a number of conferences and workshops that focus on ChatGPT and other NLP technologies. For example, the Conference on Empirical Methods in Natural Language Processing (EMNLP) (https://www.emnlp-ijcnlp2019.org/) is a widely respected conference in the field of NLP, and is held annually. The ACL workshops (https://www.aclweb.org/portal/workshops) are also a good source of information and resources about NLP, and cover a wide range of topics within the field.

www.ingramcontent.com/pod-product-compliance
Lightning Source LLC
LaVergne TN
LVHW051606050326
832903LV00033B/4381